Famous Ghosts

Susan B. Katz

Lerner Publications • Minneapolis

For Michael, who makes scary things—and everything—fun

Copyright © 2024 by Lerner Publishing Group, Inc.

All rights reserved. International copyright secured. No part of this book may be reproduced, stored in a retrieval system, or transmitted in any form or by any means—electronic, mechanical, photocopying, recording, or otherwise—without the prior written permission of Lerner Publishing Group, Inc., except for the inclusion of brief quotations in an acknowledged review.

Lerner Publications Company
An imprint of Lerner Publishing Group, Inc.
241 First Avenue North
Minneapolis, MN 55401 USA

For reading levels and more information, look up this title at www.lernerbooks.com.

Main body text set in Billy Infant Regular. Typeface provided by SparkType.

Photo Editor: Annie Zheng
Lerner team: Sue Marquis

Library of Congress Cataloging-in-Publication Data

Names: Katz, Susan B., 1971- author.
Title: Famous ghosts / Susan B. Katz.
Description: Minneapolis : Lerner Publications , [2024] | Series: Lightning bolt books - that's scary! | Includes bibliographical references and index. | Audience: Ages 6-9 | Audience: Grades 2-3 | Summary: "From La Llorona to the Bell Witch, kids will thrill to learn about all kinds of famous ghosts! Chapters cover ghosts of folklore, ghosts from history, and ghost stories told around the campfire"— Provided by publisher.
Identifiers: LCCN 2022033255 (print) | LCCN 2022033256 (ebook) | ISBN 9781728491141 (lib. bdg.) | ISBN 9781728498546 (eb pdf)
Subjects: LCSH: Ghosts—Juvenile literature.
Classification: LCC BF1461 .K38 2024 (print) | LCC BF1461 (ebook) | DDC 133.1—dc23/eng/20220715

LC record available at https://lccn.loc.gov/2022033255
LC ebook record available at https://lccn.loc.gov/2022033256

Manufactured in the United States of America
1-53045-51063-10/20/2022

Table of Contents

Ghosts! — 4

Ghosts in Folklore — 6

Ghosts of the Past — 10

Ghosts around the Campfire — 14

Fun Facts — 20

The Vanishing Hitchhiker — 21

Glossary — 22

Learn More — 23

Index — 24

Ghosts!

Have you ever heard a ghost story? When a person or animal dies, their spirit is said to live on and show up as a ghost.

Some think eerie light means a ghost is near.

Some people say ghosts are invisible. They claim ghosts make things move around a room. Others say ghosts appear as light or as white shapes.

Ghosts in Folklore

People have passed down ghost stories for thousands of years. They might tell the stories to their children or write them in books. This is called folklore.

People have been whispering tales of the Headless Horseman since the Middle Ages. They say he is a man with no head, riding a horse. They think he's looking for his missing head!

"The Legend of Sleepy Hollow" is a story about the Headless Horseman.

Bloody Mary's ghost is said to appear in mirrors.

The legend of Bloody Mary says if you say "Bloody Mary" over and over, her ghost will appear. But you have to say her name while looking in a mirror.

In Mexican folklore, La Llorona is a ghost that walks along the water at night, crying, dripping wet, and wearing white. Kids in Mexico chant her name in front of mirrors to see if they'll spot a ghost.

La Llorona, or the Weeping Woman

Ghosts of the Past

History inspires ghost stories. Some believe President Abraham Lincoln haunts the White House. Grace Coolidge and Lady Bird Johnson lived there when their husbands were president. Both said Lincoln's ghost was present.

People have claimed to see Benjamin Franklin's ghost near the American Philosophical Society in Pennsylvania. Some say a statue of Franklin that stands near the building comes to life and dances!

Benjamin Franklin was a founder of the United States.

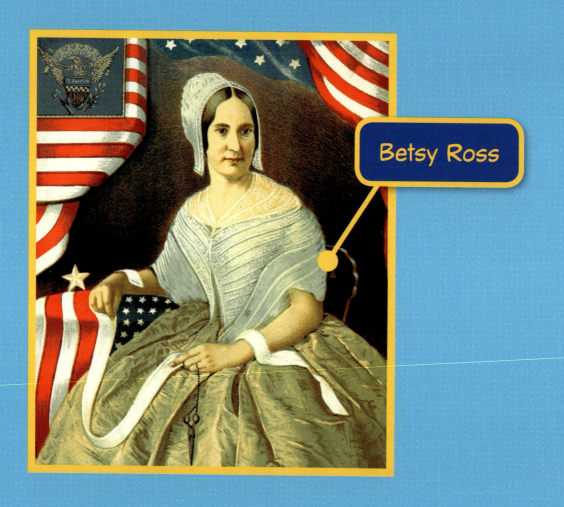

Betsy Ross

The historic Betsy Ross House is said to be the site of hauntings. The home honors Betsy Ross, who claimed to have sewed the first US flag. Different ghosts are said to haunt the home. One is Ross herself.

Visitors to the house have said they heard a woman crying. They think it's Ross's ghost. Her husband and child died while she was alive, and some say her ghost still cries for them.

Betsy Ross House

Ghosts around the Campfire

Many ghost stories are told around campfires. One is the *Flying Dutchman* tale.

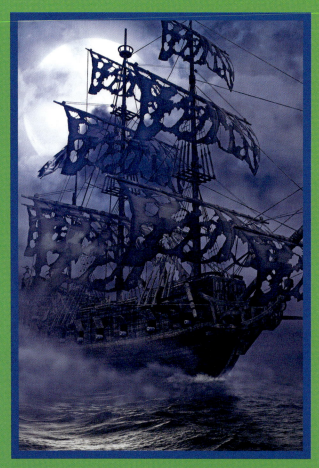

The *Flying Dutchman* is a legendary ship. People say its captain kept sailing even as people on the ship begged him to stop.

Sea lore says the *Flying Dutchman* can show up as a hazy figure or spooky light.

Legend says the *Flying Dutchman* will sail forever. Spotting the ghost ship on the high seas is thought to be bad luck.

Tales of headless ghosts are popular. Alvin Schwartz made the story of Jenny popular in a book he wrote in the 1980s.

Another campfire tale tells of a girl named Jenny who wears a green ribbon around her neck. Her boyfriend, Alfred, asks her why she wears it, but she won't tell him. In the end, when she unties the ribbon, her head falls off!

The Bell Witch Cave, near the Bell farm site

The Bell Witch tale tells of John Bell, a Tennessee farmer in the 1800s. He tried to shoot a strange farm animal, but it disappeared. Weeks later, his family's home was haunted. Their house shook. They heard scary noises.

Abandoned buildings near Bell's home

Bell also started getting sick. His face twitched. He had trouble swallowing. In 1820, he died. His family believed a witch had poisoned him.

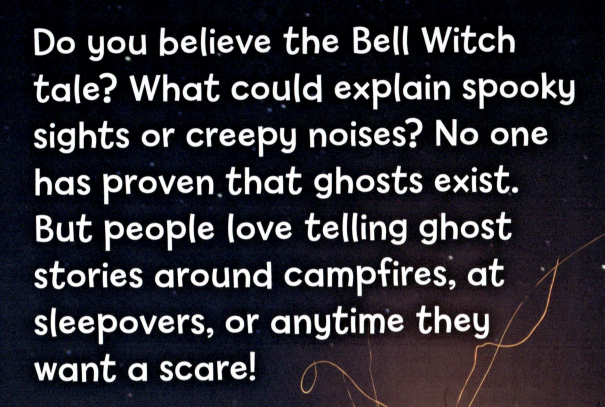

Do you believe the Bell Witch tale? What could explain spooky sights or creepy noises? No one has proven that ghosts exist. But people love telling ghost stories around campfires, at sleepovers, or anytime they want a scare!

Do you enjoy ghost stories?

Fun Facts

- Ghosts give us manners! People used to think sneezing pushed your soul out of your body. To protect the person who sneezed, someone would say, "Bless you."

- A ghost called a poltergeist is known for making knocking sounds. *Poltergeist* is German for "knocking spirit."

- Some people say a cold spot in a room means a ghost is near!

The Vanishing Hitchhiker

The Vanishing Hitchhiker is a ghost said to stand along the road, waiting for a ride. But after someone picks the ghost up, it disappears! Some say it's the ghost of someone who died. The story of the Vanishing Hitchhiker existed even before cars were invented. The story used to be about disappearing travelers on horseback or in wagons.

Glossary

folklore: a story or tale passed down from generation to generation

haunt: to visit as a ghost

inspire: to bring about

legend: a story that has been around for a long time

Middle Ages: a period, also known as Medieval Times, from the fifth to the late fifteenth centuries

Learn More

Britannica Kids: Ghost
https://kids.britannica.com/kids/article/ghost/574605

Carlson-Berne, Emma. *Ghost Hunters.* Minneapolis: Lerner Publications, 2024.

CBC Kids: 6 Spooky Things You Didn't Know about Ghosts
https://www.cbc.ca/kids/articles/monsters-101-all-about-ghosts

Kiddle: Ghost Facts for Kids
https://kids.kiddle.co/Ghost

Lassieur, Allison. *Scary Stuff.* Mankato, MN: Child's World, 2021.

Schwartz, Alvin. *In a Dark, Dark Room, and Other Scary Stories.* New York: Harper, 2017.

Index

Bell Witch tale, 17–19
Bloody Mary, 8

Flying Dutchman, 14–15
Franklin, Benjamin, 11

Headless Horseman, 7

Jenny (book character), 16

La Llorona, 9
Lincoln, Abraham, 10

Ross, Betsy, 12–13

Photo Acknowledgments

Image credits: Anastasia Skachko/Shutterstock, p. 4; Raggedstone/Shutterstock, p. 5; Tetra Images/Getty Images, p. 6; peterspiro/Getty Images, p. 7; Imagesquavondo/iStock/Getty, p. 8; Fer Gregory/Shutterstock, p. 9; John Parrot/Stocktrek Images/Getty Images, p. 10; FPG/The Image Bank/Getty Images, p. 11; Science History Images/Alamy Stock Photo, p. 12; Peter Gridley/Stockbyte/Getty Images, p. 13; Oliver Denker/Shutterstock, p. 14; Mia Stendal/Shutterstock, p. 15; AnkiHoglund/iStock/Getty Images, p. 16; Www78/Wikimedia Commons (CC BY-SA 3.0), p. 17; Brian Wilson Photography/Shutterstock, p. 18; fboudrias/Shutterstock, p. 19.

Cover image: David Wall/Getty Images.